THE SEA SHORE

M. E. ELDRIDGE

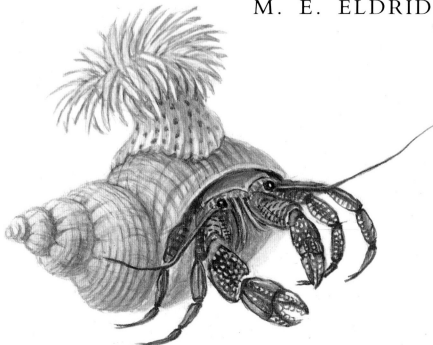

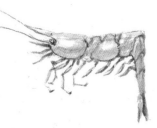

THE MEDICI SOCIETY · LONDON · 1986

On the gray stones
   where the Wild Thyme
and Sea Campion grow,
   the Wheatear displays
   the patterned feathers of his tail.

The Oystercatcher has laid her eggs near the Samphire.

The Ringed Plover makes her nest
among the coloured stones
so that no one can find it.

The pink Sea Thrift
is in full flower
and the short grass
near the Kittiwake colony
is blue with the flowers
of the Spring Squill.

Sea Holly and Sea Convolvulus
grow in the sand
where the Black-headed Gulls gather.

In the summer
Wrasse swim close to the shore
above the Sea Urchins and Starfish.

The Oystercatcher

can open Mussel shells

with its strong red beak.

In the rock pools
there are Starfish

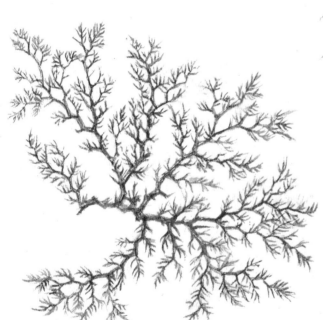

and Sea Anemones,
Shore Crabs and small fishes.

The Puffins like to stand in groups and look out to sea.

In autumn
there are Gray Seal pups
on the beach,
and shells and Carrageen
and Mermaids Purses
are carried ashore
by the rough waves.

When there is frost and snow
birds from the moors and the hills,
Curlew and Lapwing, gather on the shore.

Printed in England. ISBN 0 85503 091 7   B20